Writing Your Fund-Raising Case Statement

Process, Not Creative Agony

By Walter Donway

Romantic Revolution Books

Writing Your Fund-Raising Case Statement

Writing Your Fundraising Case Statement: Process, Not Creative Agony
Copyright 2017 © Walter Donway
ISBN-13: 978-1978459274
ISBN-10: 1978459270
All rights reserved. By payment of the required fees, you have been granted the nonexclusive, non-transferable right to access and read the text of this book. No part of this text may be reproduced, transmitted, downloaded, decompiled, reverse engineered, or stored in or introduced into any information storage and retrieval system, in any form or by any means, whether electronic or mechanical, now known or hereinafter invented, without the express permission of the copyright owner.
Romantic Revolution Books
279 Stephen Hands Path
East Hampton, NY 11937
WDonway@Gmail.com

Dedicated

*To the late, legendary Burr Gibson,
pioneer of the modern capital campaign,
who got me into the business*

Writing Your Fund-Raising Case Statement

Walter Donway

The author is a professional writer who has specialized in writing capital- and annual-fundraising case statements for several decades. As a communications associate of Marts & Lundy, among the world's premier fund-raising consulting firms, he has completed more than 100 successful case statements, prospectuses, brochures, and major proposals. His clients have been some of the country's foremost universities, academic medical centers, hospitals, biomedical research organizations, disease advocacy groups, independent secondary schools, performing arts organizations, environmental organizations, museums, fellowship organizations, libraries, churches, and others. A partial list of clients can be found in the Appendix.

Writing Your Fund-Raising Case Statement

In addition, he has been a program officer for
the Commonwealth Fund, a New York City
foundation in the fields of health care, health
care research, biomedical research, medical
education, and international fellowships. He
was program director for education, director of
communications, director of the Dana Press,
and founding editor of the quarterly journal,
Cerebrum: The Dana Forum on Brain Science,
for the Charles A. Dana Foundation, a New
York City foundation in the fields of liberal arts
education, support for academic medical
centers, and, now, advocacy for funding of
research in neuroscience.

He provides fundraising and other writing
services and can be reached at WDonway
@Gmail.com or through Marts & Lundy. He
works out of New York City and eastern Long
Island, but is available to travel, including
abroad for English language organizations.

Writing Your Fund-Raising Case Statement

Writing Your Fund-Raising Case Statement

Contents

Writing Your Fund-Raising Case Statement

Process, not creative agony

> *Between the conception*
> *and the creation*
> *between the emotion*
> *and the response*
> *falls the Shadow.*
> -- T.S. Eliot

Do *not* begin your fund-raising statement, or use anywhere within it, any quotation of poetry. Unless you are the American Academy of Poets. It is not poetry that moves your potential contributor; it is demonstration of the value you deliver for the philanthropic dollar. It is the contributor's conviction that the values your organization works to achieve are those that the contributor wants to promote—or even, it may be, holds dear. Drafting a case for new financial resources is a task undertaken by tens of thousands of nonprofit organizations every year. It is vital to the future of their mission, sometimes to their survival. It need not be—but all too often is--a gauntlet of creative angst.

Of course, the job can be farmed out to a professional writer. Any fundraising firm will do it. Freelancers will do it for less and call it "writing." The fees are not significant if your organization plans a multi-million-dollar campaign.

What often happens, I find, is that someone in the organization is assigned or volunteers to draft the case. Plenty of time; it is not needed for months, perhaps. But the writer puts off the dreaded encounter with the blank screen until the case must be done— soon! And then the psychic pressure is unmanning. The organization cries out to a professional writer and explains that it has only two weeks until the board meeting at which the draft must be presented. There always is a writer who will do it. Now, the organization does not negotiate the fee. It pays up. One director of development came clean, telling me: "I find this embarrassing. We couldn't write our case statement in three months and we are giving you one week."

The message is not that you cannot write your case statement. It is that the job is not to await inspiration, the creative moment. It is to follow a known process that requires intelligence, diligence, persistence, but not elusive inspiration. Inspiration is not how professionals manage to produce case statement after case statement, day in and day out, good enough to get the money.

This brief guide can be used in at least two ways. It can help your organization to draft its own case statement—avoiding the agony by making the process systematic, not "creative." Or, let me say, by reducing the "creative" writing to the editing phase. Or, it can be a guide to understanding—and monitoring—the work of a professional writer. Combining the two functions, it can be a way to draft your own case until you reach the point where a professional writer can give it a bit of the pizzazz and polish you want.

My chief message to you, then, is that much of the preparation of your case statement can be reduced to steps that do not require "inspiration" of the writer. And that creative step, which is to make the case in fresh, passionate, urgent prose, is far less daunting when all preparatory steps have been taken.

I should not say this, perhaps, as a guy who has made a living drafting case statements in high style; but if you honestly, fully state your case, as specified below, then even clear, work-a-day, business-letter prose may be good enough. If you demonstrate that your product is excellent, you need not sing its praises like a bard at the king's table. (If you insist on stylistic grace and rhetorical passion, then I am your man. My avocation is writing poetry, novels, and memoirs.)

Answer these questions

What questions, in what order, should your case statement address? The indispensable core, the skeleton, is the logic of the case for funds. By that, I mean a statement of unadorned propositions leading to a conclusion. If the information required for this argument is not available, then your organization is not ready for a fundraising campaign. If a campaign for survival cannot be postponed, then a case *can* be developed, but not as described, here. The case you need is essentially for *start-up* funding: funding of a "premise" or a "promise" or a "dream."

Returning to the logic of the case, these are questions to answer. You are not concerned with style, or creativity, or inspiration, right now. Just in recording information.

- What is the mission of your organization?

- Why is the mission important? Who is served in what ways?

- Why is the mission especially important *today*?

- What is your organization's record of fulfilling its mission? What are its achievements--quantified, generalized, exemplified?

- What funding has made possible these achievements? Endowment? Annual fundraising? Income-producing activities? Government grants?

- What is your organization's relative position today in its field, its standing among its "competitors" or peers?

- What challenges does your organization face, now? What needs press upon its field? What funding stringencies? What unmet needs? What unrealized opportunities?

- What are your organization's plans for meeting these challenges? By

- means of what goals, programs, activities?

- How have these plans been formulated and vetted (e.g., by the director? Trustees? A special committee)?

- How will the future be different if your organization meets these challenges? What will be achieved? Who will be served? How will the world change?

- What specific dollars are needed to meet the challenges? Funding for what? How much? When?

- What is the organization's plan for obtaining the resources? A capital-campaign? An annual campaign?

- Where does planning for your campaign stand, right now?

- What do you ask your supporters, potential supporters, to do right now?

- Why is it important that they act right now?

Who should answer the questions?

Anyone around an organization for a few years can improvise answers to some of questions without leaving his or her desk or picking up a phone. Of course, you know your mission! You know your needs all too well! And your challenges!

But to answer the questions in a way that prepares for your campaign, the case must speak with the *voice of your organization.* Can't the head, or president, or chairman of your organization speak with that voice. Perhaps, but that is still one voice. Can the chairman of a university's trustees speak of the excitement of learning at the university as well as its faculty members? Students?

Alumni? Can the chairman of the museum's board speak of what art can mean to the viewer in the same way that the curator can?

More reliable, I think, is to *listen* to many voices. Typically, I have prepared myself by reading a literal box full of publications and documents (and, more recently, taking notes from the Web site), then gone "on site" for a dozen or more intensive interviews with development staff, executives, trustees, program staff, students (or performers, or clients, or users), and sometimes potential contributors (but the latter usually come after the case statement is drafted).

Another way, complementary to interviews, is to get the organization's players around a table to brainstorm answers to the questions.

To ask each question and listen to the interaction of responses, pushing with questions for still more thoughtful responses. Around that table are executives and administrators, staff, but also clients (e.g., students, alumni), current funders, neighbors (if the organization impacts on them), and even observant outsiders (e.g., friendly local media representatives).

The needed answers are factual, demonstrable, the result of due process (trustee decisions), documentable (planning documents, budgets), attested (statements from those served), exemplified (successful cases, instances, individuals), and compelling (logical in the context of the case).

Reaching the person, not the "donor"

A special kind of answer, viewed by some as the soul of the case statement, is a "story" of how your organization fulfilled its mission in a specific, concrete case involving real individuals whose lives were changed. Every organization has such stories. Listen for them, provoke them with requests for examples of claimed successes, and write them down.

Because the logic of your case--the strict argument for value provided, value to be delivered--is inseparable from a reader's emotional response to values. We experience our values, often, on the emotional level, with feelings of nostalgia, gratitude, identification, hope, an urge to reciprocate, and an urge to identify with an organization or cause by attaching our name or some loved one's name to the organization and its work.

The temptation of the "insider," at times, is to capture those emotions by means of evocative words charged with feeling. There is a place for that, certainly. But our most powerful emotions are evoked not by language, however eloquent, but by experiences of ourselves or of people like us. Stories move us. Whether people experience what we are experiencing or experience what we fear—or hope—for ourselves, it is people's lives that engage us.

In the end, we identify with an organization or a cause and make it our own--or we do not. If there is a creative aspect to the case statement, once the logical argument is in place, it is the ability to tell a story in terms that move the emotions of the potential contributor—not against logic, but as passionate incarnation of that logic.

If you must choose between a logician and a poet to prepare your case statement, always choose the logician. Once you have a case that compels that rational mind, poets may have their say. It does not work in reverse.

The hot seat: sitting down to write it

With your homework done—the matrix of questions filled—and with a feeling for stories that enliven the logic—you sit down to draft the case. This is not the time to abandon logic and try to write the opening lines of an immortal opera. You are simply putting the answers to the questions in plain prose arranged as a narrative statement of the case. This is just the next step in the job.

First, state the entire case in one sentence. Your organization, now, has identified its priorities for the future--to continue to accomplish this or that, meeting the pressing needs of this group or that—and to

make that future a reality seeks
$00,000,000 in a three-year capital
fundraising campaign. You have
encapsulated the case. Now, explain to the
reader what it is all about with the answers
to the questions you have obtained.

The next paragraph states the campaign
objective in less formal, moving terms, and
assures the reader that the trustees, the
board, the leadership have thoroughly
planned and approved the campaign. I call
this "due process."

The first subsection might explain who you
are, how you began, and why your role is
so important.

The next subsection might zero-in on who
you are *today*, who you serve now, what

goals you are advancing. This is your brief portrait of a relevant, efficacious, growing organization that is meeting an urgent need.

The next subsection might explain the challenges that you face: the continuing needs, the unmet needs, the aspirations, the good that could be accomplished, the dream.

The next subsection might explain your plans to meet these challenges: the new initiatives, the even better programs, the indispensable facilities, all the investments in continued and growing success.

The next subsection might enlarge upon the planning—the due process—of the proposed campaign: how all the organization's stakeholders have had their part in reaching consensus about the future.

The next subsection might explain what you are asking the reader to do right now. Respond to a survey? Estimate his or her ability to contribute to the campaign goal? Make a gift?

The final subsection might be a brief restatement of what success of the campaign will mean for your mission and the importance of each contributor's decision to be part of that future.

Revising to liberate a little passion

Your case is drafted. But every draft must be revised, right?

Have you *stated the logic of the case* in clear, straightforward prose? Are the transitions between subsections logical? Does the case sound like one rational mind communicating with another? Nothing is more important. If a potential major contributor can poke holes in your logic, see contradictions, identify exaggerations, then even poetry won't save you.

On Madison Avenue there is a legend about two fundraising professionals sitting on a bench in Central Park on a glorious spring day. On the bench across the walk sits a man alone holding up a sign: "I am blind." There is a cup in his hand, but few passersby are dropping in a coin. Finally, one man says to the other: "I can add four words to that sign and triple the guy's success."

"Sure, why don't you ask him?" So, the ad man walks over, talks with the blind man, who reaches into his pocket for the magic marker someone used to make the sign for him. The ad man takes it and above what the man has on his sign, adds: "It is spring, and…"

Now, the sign reads: "It is spring, and I am blind."

Unreliable legend has it that the blind man's cup runneth over.

Every cause, mission, and organization has a vocabulary of commitment and empathy. Biomedical research is urgent, rigorous, dedicated, crucial to patients, gives hope, brings relief… An independent secondary school is academically excellent, challenging, nurturing, diverse, builds character, and realizes potential…

There is nothing cynical or cliched about this. These organization exist for those goals and values and they should say so. Editing the case statement, you look for the places where the terms used to characterize your organization belong. "Inclusive?" "Highly selective?" "Elite?" Each has its place. But in the end, you want the reader to feel your hope, excitement, deep concern, passion for progress, dedication to a cause. The words added to the blind man's sign are effective if now passersby identify with him. They are enjoying a heart-lifting spring day with its palette of bright colors. The blind man, too, senses the glory about him—but never will see it. He shares their humanity, but not their good fortune—and many wish that they could share that with him. too. So, they share their pocket money with him.

But adjectives have their limits. The best writers of case statements, today, know that—always and everywhere--the reader is interested in people. The writer knows that this means stories about people and their motives, values, problems, struggles, and triumphs. What are the stories that in few sentences capture the human dimension of your organization and its values?

You want your reader to feel that when he gives you the financial resources he has earned he has gained an ally in his quest for his own dearest values. That is where the logic and passion of your case statement come together to express the same message. It is not "hype" that you seek, but a recreation on the page, in words, of what is possible if your reader animates your mission. And that no dollar he contributes will be wasted.

Revising part II: the "buy in"

The writer has summoned all his logic, integrity, and talent to state the case. Now, he must disown it. He must offer—nay, urge--ownership of it by the entire organization with whose it speaks. He invites the organization to assess, criticize, attack, revise what he has written and feels is perfect. He listens to every comment— praiseful, hurtful, helpful, carping, subversive—and incorporates it into his case to the extent he can do so *without compromising its integrity.*

He gratefully accepts recommendations that improve what he has done—and there will be some. He graciously acknowledges recommendations that would not help the case—and makes changes that are optional. He thanks everyone for contributing to make the case, the true voice of the organization.

If it is a full case statement, not a prospectus, your organization will use it for years as the basis, or reference document, for proposals, letters of proposal, speeches, and, when the campaign concludes its silent phase and goes public, as the basis for the campaign brochure. Because the case has been checked and vetted and approved, what is drawn from it will not have to be approved all over again, each time it is used. All communications will be consistent in facts, logic, figures, and tone.

Now, the writer seeks anonymity. If he succeeds, the organization has claimed the case statement as its own. For the duration of the campaign—perhaps three years or more—the organization will represent itself to the world in the case statement.

One footnote on this matter. In almost every organization there will be a top executive, usually on the board of trustees, who in his business demands that all memos to him not exceed one page. He tells the writer that no important potential contributor wants more than one page. What the *hell* to do? I have encountered this, of course, and what I do is say: "You know, you are right. We need that one page."

And I go and write a precis of the case, an executive summary, that "says it all" on one page. That becomes an optional first page of the case where it might help. Its title is "Executive Summary" and the last line is "A full statement of the case is presented in the following pages."

We're going to hire a professional anyway

You've convinced us. This "easy" approach to the case statement sounds like the punishment of Job. We can afford the luxury of a professional writer. I mean, aren't there *some* benefits?

Sure, there are. I point them out all the time. A professional writer, especially with a fund-raising firm, has read and written perhaps dozens of case statements. I have written more than 100. I have solved a lot of problems and have those solutions in my tool belt. Also, I have had my case statements (in these instances called "prospectuses," used in surveys of potential contributors and seen the compiled results of their responses—always including some questions about the adequacy of the case.

A professional writer is an outsider to your organization. Indeed, he may have heard of your organization only when he got the assignment. As an outsider, he may see more readily and clearly the big picture, the salient issues, the attractive features, and the "reason for being" of your organization.

Also, by the nature of the assignment, he is "testing" the case he writes on himself; he is trying, first, to sell himself on your campaign. In a sense, your case is passing its first test.

A professional writer is likely to work fulltime on the case, without the obligations of everyday work of someone inside the organization. This means an intense focus, a concentration on the draft, that does underpin a certain creativity—including, I admit, even dreaming about the case. And, more simply, the job gets done on deadline.

In the stage of revision, the professional writer can accept criticism perhaps more easily than someone in the organization who must hear his case criticized by his colleagues, his boss, his friends. I was retained through Marts & Lundy to write the case statement for a school where my son was finishing his nursery school year. When she realized I was a parent, the head of school asked if I would write the case *"pro bono."* I declined; in fact, I had to decline, this was a Marts & Lundy client. I completed the case and submitted it; she called, declaring it perfect and invited me to its "coming out party" a couple weeks later. On that day, I heard that my son would not be admitted to the school's kindergarten— not suitable. I arrived that evening at the "party" for the case and thoroughly startled the head, who assumed I would not show up. I am a professional.

And when it comes to "disowning" the case, becoming anonymous so that the organization owns its statement, that is automatic when the professional writer shakes hands all around and walks out the door with his check.

These are a few of the reasons that America is served by dozens of major fundraising consultancies, now often with offices abroad, that make good livings for their top professionals. The modern capital campaign was not inevitable; it was invented, step by step, by a relatively few leaders in fundraising, including my erstwhile colleague, CEO of Marts & Lundy, Burr Gibson. Today, tools of the campaign go far beyond the wisdom and experience of the consultant. Computer screening for potential prospects, for example, has become an entire department of major consulting firms.

 What is the single greatest concern that organizations have about using a professional writer? I think it is that the writer will not grasp what is unique (a better term is "distinctive") about the organization. The writer will view it, for example, as a liberal arts college, or Ivy League university, or university medical center, and have a template on hand for that kind of case. It will be "cookie cutter." I can understand the temptation; original work is tough and never is without some anxiety because there is no known outcome. The outcome may surprise and please even the writer.

How can you be sure you get an original, not a "cc" or "bcc"? You can't. You check out the writer's work, make clear and explicit that your priority is that your organization-not a generic product—exists on the page, give the writer enough time, and connect him with people in your organization known for their feelings about it. And, during the stages of revision, when the existentialist angst of the blank page is not facing you, add telling details, a story, a term evocative in your organization. At my own alma mater, Brown University, every graduating glass passes through Van Wickle Gates and marches down College Hill. It doesn't require Leo Tolstoy to realize that the gates, and the hill, are cherished icons of this university and only this university.

The professional writer works within, and is supported, by his colleagues in the firm. Be sure that they also will support a case statement writer within your organization if you have fundraising counsel at the time the statement is drafted. But laying it on the line with a colleague is different from dealing with a writer who also is the client. I know that many firms, including Marts & Lundy, give clients an option for the case statement: let the firm do the job or give it to someone in your organization and let the firm rewrite and revise it as necessary. The costs, of course, are very different.

A "professional," technically, is one paid for what he or she does. Another definition is that a professional always produces work up to a standard. Not necessarily brilliant, but competent. I identify with that. I have written better and worse case statements. I think the worst were competent, got the money. The best are beyond my ability fully to explain. My message, here, is that it doesn't matter. It is a distraction in producing a case statement that works.

Don't hesitate to undertake preparation of your own case if that makes financial sense. At worst, you will collect the answers to the questions I have set forth and perhaps reduce considerably how many days a professional writer will require to finish the job. Or, with so much information and insight in hand, and organized, tackling the writing might seem less daunting to a writer in your organization.

How sweet it is!

I am going to take my own advice and conclude with a story. I undertook to write a case statement for a national association committed to supporting research and care for a major disease. The campaign goal was in seven figures, so the "survey case statement," or prospectus, was long, perhaps eight single-spaced pages, with a few charts and other visuals. It was packed with challenging information about progress on the disease and complexities of research support with a leviathan— government— swimming in the same direction. It evoked a vision of what progress--not success, just progress--would mean for men and women suffering and dying with the disease.

The report was revised, accepted, formatted, and sent to about 40 potential prospects, who would be surveyed about their response to the case.

The day after the case was shipped by overnight express, a contributor from Dallas called the organization's president. He said he was so excited and moved by the plans and prospects set forth in the case, that he wanted to pledge a million dollars. I would not kid you. His wife had died of the disease, so, naturally, he already brought plenty of passion to the cause. But the case statement became a catalyst for that passion and moved him to action.

How sweet it is!

The end

Appendix

A Partial List of Clients Served

Examples of most recent projects:

American Alzheimer's association (preliminary capital campaign case statement), Cato Institute (annual fundraising appeal), Chelsea Day School (campaign survey prospectus), Learning Success Network (survey prospectus), McDonogh School (survey statement), King Fahd University of Saudi Arabia (fundraising campaign brochures).

Examples of range of projects:

American Ballet Theatre, Baldwin
School, Bank Street College of
Education, Brooks School, Cambridge
University, Concordia University,
Convent of the Sacred Heart (NY),
The Culinary Institute of America,
Dartmouth-Hitchcock Medical Center,
Deerfield Academy, DePaul
University, Embry-Riddle
Aeronautical University, Fairleigh
Dickinson University, Flintridge
Preparatory School, Florida State
University Foundation, Hockaday
School, Inova Health System, J. Paul
Getty Museum, Hartford Symphony,
Hospital for Special Surgery, Lehigh
University, Lupus Research Institute,
The Madeira School, Mills College,

Morton Arboretum, National Geographic Society, Nature Conservancy (national), New York City Ballet, New York Historical Society, New York University Medical Center, North Shore University Hospital, Quincy University, Parrish Art Museum, Parsons School of Design, Philadelphia Museum of Art, Philadelphia Zoo, The Pingree School, Roger Williams University, Saint Anselm College, South Florida "Carnival" Center for the Performing Arts, Spence School, Sonoma Academy, NYU Stern School, Syracuse University, Texas A&M University, United Negro College Fund, Union Theological Seminary, University at Albany, University at

Buffalo, University of Missouri at
Rolla, University of Toronto, Wake
Forest Baptist Medical Center, Webb
Institute, Williams College, The
Williston Northampton School, World
Monuments Fund.

Other projects:

Achilles International, Berkeley-
Carroll School, Fifth Avenue
Presbyterian Church, LEAD Program
in Business, Madison Avenue
Presbyterian Church, Manhattan
Institute, New York Public Library,
Overlook Medical Center, Salzburg
Seminar in American Studies.

Notes

www.ingramcontent.com/pod-product-compliance
Lightning Source LLC
Chambersburg PA
CBHW060810260726
48660CB00002B/875